lan(d)guage

Caitlin Press Inc.
8100 Alderwood Road,
Halfmoon Bay, BC V0N 1Y1
www.caitlin-press.com

Text and cover designed by the house
Cover image Ken Belford
Printed in Canada

Caitlin Press Inc. acknowledges financial support from the Govern-
ment of Canada through the Book Publishing Industry Development
Program and the Canada Council for the Arts, and from the Province
of British Columbia through the British Columbia Arts Council and
the Book Publisher's Tax Credit.

**Canada Council
for the Arts**

**Conseil des Arts
du Canada**

BRITISH COLUMBIA
ARTS COUNCIL

Library and Archives Canada Cataloguing in Publication

Belford, Ken, 1946-
    Lan(d)guage : a sequence in poetics / Ken Belford.

ISBN 978-1-894759-29-8

    I. Title. II. Title: Language.

PS8503.E47L35 2008   C811'.54   C2008-904823-7

lan(d)guage

a sequence of poetics

KEN BELFORD

for Karle —
Ken Belford

Caitlin Press

for Si

Say you are walking along
and turn off
onto the wrong trail.
Say you see caragana, raspberries,
nettles along a split rail fence. Then
an eagle arcs into view,
and the impulse moves on,
a coalition of memories
where the winner takes all.
The laws of nature change.
Consciousness, if it is at all,
is physical, that is, it's poker-faced,
or dog-faced. Kissed all over by neurons,
the sea slugs of memory share ideas.

In the presence of blood and lymph, animals forgive
more quickly than men and live next to us
above the level of the sea. Fish browse
in pastures. The fielder returns the ball in play.
Next could be someone else,
the queen of horses, anyone else, a hayfoot
or a strawfoot, a pair of polymorphic likeness's
with short necks and wings.
And there are traps. Those who must have animals
are easily startled or hurt by too much mother
or too much father. The journey
of young men can end in a different place,
where their minds thicken and harden.
The largest predators are never seen.
These are the types: Those who must have animals
with them, those who lie back of form, those
who bring instructions and supplies,
those who are a type of something
and independent from other kinds,
illusionists who say they make reality
and those who tried.

I slept beside a grizzly, each of us unaware
of the other, and when I awakened, heard
his breath next to mine. Time began for me
in that instant when I arose and saw him
sleeping there with a salmonberry leaf
on his head. No longer alone, all things since
are altered by that switch. What else is there
to know, each of us asleep and happy?
But he awakened just then and barreled off
into the brush, toward everything necessary.
At that moment everything I knew left me
and now a new world has taken place.
It comes to the same thing—astonishment
that this should happen at all. But I heard
him breathe, and saw him make tracks
before I could think. To see this thing
was not horrendous, and to see it go
was not delightful. Nothing meaningful
occurred, but time started with a big bear.
This is not about anything, but I'm waiting
for some thing to come up behind me
in the night. I'm like something else now,
and every breath I take anticipates
that moment I want again and again.

Nothing can be done to save you of poetry.
Poetry is one hundred percent communicable.
Even one poem is enough to begin a cycle.
Ingestion of infected poetry results in
permanent death, but injecting poetry
directly into a dead brain is useless.
Meat inspectors, when not looking for lesions,
laugh at the poem and spit at the poet.
Poets possess no powers of regeneration—
poems that are damaged, stay damaged.
Poems travel through the bloodstream,
from their point of entry to the brain.
Not waterborne nor airborne, poems use the cells
of the frontal lobe for replication. This is why
no poetry occurs in nature. Warning
against an act of poetry would be useless,
as the only people to listen would be unconcerned
for their own safety. A poem is safe to handle
within hours of the death of its host.
Children have been infected by brushing their wounds
against those of a poem. In the pastoral areas
of the east and west, studies have shown
that institutions can sense and will reject
an infected poet one hundred percent of the time.
Unless someone teaches a course that feeds on living,
human poets, there will be no life in their poems,
no warmth in their words.

There's a fictional literacy called access.
Some of us get there by going
a different way. Some doors work,
some don't. People used to think narrative
depicted subjects but now it's about
the gestures of avatars. Old meaning is
the assimilation of the words of others.
It's a kind of camera surveillance, so
I alter my behaviour when I'm shifting
around town. When asked, I say
my server is down. In the old oral texts,
results are rewarded, and the words
made flesh. Teachers point at the page
and point at the text. I mean, this looks
like a poem on a page but there's a world
of difference. My narrative is waves of meaning
crashing through a watery code. Sometimes
meaning is stupid and reading is painful.
Clusters of tiny, new perceptions shift
and turn at once and I don't know
how it works, but I can see it. I can see you
in the river and as crazy as it sounds,
I can hear your cries for help.

Snakes awaken, dogs howl and
I pick up the signals animals do.
Some days there's a lot of bleeding,
other days, no bleeding at all.
Sometimes it doesn't work
then after a while it starts again.
Some days there's chaos in the operating room,
days when drugs won't stimulate the heart
and earthworms emerge in winter.
Other days I'm aware of the contractions
of the smallest hearts, a spot of blood
with a pumping heart. Other people
have other theories. At the end of things,
when chickens fidget, it depends
on who you talk to, who has a headache
and who sees it coming.

Nature becomes structureless when
catastrophe occurs and an animal disappears.
Then we experience a time of transient chaos
before another attractor in crisis is found.
Say I was happy until my wife ran over me
and now I live with another. It's like that,
having to do with the distance between centers.
I guess I could characterize my past as chaotic
but others might not see it that way.
So my faith has flaws now and the movies
don't move right. The forms move, not
the pictures, and I won't be placing bets
on the wrong idea or the future of individual
models on the fashion pages. I thought
the future might never happen, but it did.
Extensions are dimensions and there are
not many forms. Most of them look alike.
Short poems are modeled by portraits
of phrases, whereas long poems run on
perceptions based on the food chain
and the weather. I forget the tangles
and think of harmony and resonance
when my sympathy string is pulled.

Poems flow from top down, and
analysis, in the conditional voice
of the critic, is filtered from the bottom
up, with a frame-to-frame separation
that drives me around the bend.
Long rivers collect and tributaries
subtract. In flood, the clicks we hear
are the moving stones that fill the holes.
We pay for properties with boundaries
to see the story told. A poem is a lifeline
thrown at a dreamboat destined to sink.
I'm looking for the smallest bits of meaning.
First I stop to pick up your clothes and
then I put them down in another place.
In the background scene of the image,
the river surges from the flow fields,
and the boundaries of the smallest
meanings eventually add up to a subject
that knows it's readers too well.

Publishing is an urban industry
designing poetry products about
how we tell the close-to-my-heart
stamping stories of our lives.
Based in Chicago, hog butcher
to the world, Poetry Butcher sells
printable scrapbooking pages for
beginning and established poets.
Sold exclusively at Scrap Boys
right there in the butcher shop,
these embellishments are collections
of fresh meat called meaningful books
preserving family memories.

My first marriage was a closed curve
and together we travelled into the past,
wasting time. Time passes more slowly
at the bottom of a well. We could not be
brought together. Today I went back
in time and deleted my old love poems,
and kept my past and present separate,
between the knower and the known,
and remembered when time was passing
and nothing was happening.
The accumulated reader paradox states
whenever multitudes of poetry tourists wish
to attend a reading, the poets of quietude say
there are no such readers, no such love.
When the past collapses, and things seem
too late, and we think first love never happened,
when it seems nothing in the past is real, then
we know there is no paradox in reading from
back to front when we open a book of poems.
Not machines, but faster than light,
poems allow for time travel, but it is
only possible to go as far back in the past
as remembering we could never exist,
even though everything is possible.
The meter of a poem is consistent and
can never be changed because one does
not have full control of the poem.
New poems can be copies of old ones

with changes caused by time, and any event
that changes a line, creates a new one.
New poems are flexible and subject to change
but published poems are change resistant.
A small change in a published poem
will alter the immediate future, whereas
a large change in a known poem will
alter the distant future. The date of
an unpublished poem is easily changed
because the lines are fluid.
Attempts to travel into the past
to change a poem are possible, provided
the changes do not interfere with the present,
but the poet should know there is no possibility
of returning to the present to witness the change.
As soon as one attempts to write a poem,
one undergoes time travel. This is
the McKinnon effect. If poets write stories,
readers encounter slippage, which prevents them
from reaching the end of the poem. This is
the Budde effect. A poet who travels into
the past to change his grandfather poem
is snapped back into the present the moment
the lines are changed. This is the Bowering effect.

The unfilled level above the title band
is the conduction band. In the poem
there are no forbidden gaps and
what is added and what is replaced
fills the lattice spacing of the crystal.
Compound poets are made of common
examples. Semiconductor poets are of
the same type and are bound together
by bonds. The Rumsfelt neuron is
a random mutation of a quantum bug.
Ordinarily an error, it's linked
to a super-text of images and displays
with a shift in funding faked right in.
Particles like me are caught in a trap
where the reagents have been sequenced
like ripples in a pond. The best I can do is
migrate to the wall but I'd like to switch over
to the flip side and be a transistor that
could crack these disorders and
circulate the bullets back.

Reading first person shooter poems is like
looking at a video of a dead farm animal.
The game engine's narrative is based
on a privileged model of choice and
direction, passed through a fear-based
filter, out of which meaning is access
to engine code. It gets me all frissony.
I'm an original but I'm not perfect.
This is a copy and that's why it's worthless.
There's a couple of real problems here.
The first is the artificial notions of originality
and the second is a poetry of distributable
solutions. There are copies of the game
everywhere, but I'm keeping the poem
in play, and that says something about
the piss-poor joystick movement, forgeries,
and the unintended application ever
since the original .exe game was lost.

Seeing is not believing when love goes wrong
in the flashback scenes and I want to see you
again, to see your face in the crowd. From what
precedes, one concludes. I lived before in a surrounding
without surprises. You don't need to know anything
about complexity theory to fall in love. But now,
weak forms are converted into strong forms and
before I believed in you, I believed in another.
At moments such as this, content swims backstroke
and saying shifts to belief. There is no place where
it all comes together. I lost track of the correct order
of the frames and now it seems meaning, or pictures,
or language, is occupied with sequence judgments.
There is no master, no judge, no authorized moment
to measure content. There are different versions
spliced together in the cutting room, always lined up,
always backed up, and I'm ready to run it through again.

And in the spring I was dark wood in a rich soil,
dark skinned like bread made from dark flour.
I lived in a building faced with stone.
By fall I was a polished stick, a silly,
incompetent old man. I'd taken a beating.
I'm an awkward bugger that doesn't fit.
An inch here in the now isn't an inch
there in the past. I come to all my
relational now children by chance,
knowing there's a rooted bias in the game
and one is more popular than the others.
It seems the frontiers are strata—or is it
the other way around? At the end of time,
the pages are sorted in reverse. If you were
to put yourself in my place, and I borrowed
memories from the outside, who would
unfold them and who would know me?
Who would know these happy old sockeye are
time capsules coming back, for example, now?

Oh anadromous love below
the lateral line, grow quickly in the sea.
They die in the other Fraser River
or off-channel in the Iliamna
and then the sculpins decline.
I saw the island beaches,
mean pink salmon returns
and the Meziadin falls.
And I had time and transportation
back then, between early and late,
before vessels were restricted,
before hatcheries, when we were
planting sockeye in the basin,
in the heart of Seattle.

Animals are not good to eat, but good to think.
Part bird, part fish, they ascend my river.
Metamorphosis is voluntary,
words turn into poetry, the salmon die
and their families are abundant
before they migrate to the sea.
In farming and tourism, animals are symbols.
The use of animals in the classroom
is as old as consciousness.
At the end of the run, winter begins
when the river is pure again.
Sometimes, when I read poetry,
I think of the observation of caged animals.
Little is known when meaning migrates
to another poem and language shifts.
Countless bodies passing through in the river.

And some can fly, and some
can swim, and predators are
usually more dangerous
than falls, but when a cow trips,
falling takes on meaning,
and big animals know
the immediacy of gravity.
It seems the ratio of words
about cattle to words about size
has nothing to do with truth,
but runs parallel to that moment
when we step out of sequence.
If you slice anything thin
enough, everything disappears
into waves and rays.
Meaning never gets far
from the sweetheart deal,
and we make poems about
comparable coherences,
with a bias towards topics,
and rummage for rules
in the immediate world.

When a boy, I talked with grasses, as boys do,
and I knew the intelligence and syntax of leaves.
Now I am older, and by day I do homework,
but by night I'm Spark the Pollinator.
I will not die within this year.
Touched by meaning, I took plant words in
through my nose and my skin.
I still can't say what meaning is.
But trees think big. Called to the plants
in this time of invaders, I have cut my last tree.
And when one of them is ill,
or is girdled by an outsider who isn't thinking ahead,
as plants do, when plants are threatened and remember
transgressions, and curl their leaves, when
invaders enter wetlands, and the wild plants calculate
where to go, and with whom, it's then
the Blackwater remembers me. Plants plan
and make decisions we call medicines
and lipids but really they heal and create community
so that none of us are alone.
Pollinators produce results that are
not predictable, and although plants wonder
about the future, there's no sense in trying
to fool a plant into thinking it's July
when it's really September.

Trees make shadows
and alternative environments
are fragmented by disturbances.
Water snakes and anglers come here.
Strong stories with strong tails
and long, broad gills are going
and now I walk around town
remembering the big trees.
Rainbows have a strong fidelity
to wood-formed pools in the fall.
Matrix dams last for years.
The bigger the trees, the better.
The loss of the old growth
makes huge disturbances.
Rivers need trees that don't move
until everything moves.
Complex flow, heterogeneous zone.
Look around—trees in the water
and trees on the ground
make new sediment terraces
and a certain kind of fish
in a certain kind of water
forms around obstructions
that cause friction.

The sand snakes of the America-to-be
will thrive with their streamlined heads
and minimized friction, but today the pressure
of implantation comes at a price, and
the fractured leads that connect to my heart
face west. What we don't hurt will know us.
Only the unprotected listen to poetry,
and the density of objects, multiplied
by a fictional audience would not be
a cabin, but more likely a low relief wrinkle
on top of a hill. Given the larger numbers to
the south, and a few close calls (one in March,
another in May,) and knowing how out on
the plateau, the ground waters flow outward
from faults, I think I'll tell my own story
of the steps, of how I got out of the land,
how it wasn't quick, how it wasn't easy.

My home was dangerous. A carrier of conflict,
I sought safety in a strange land, and lived
for a while with nothing over my head.
The living conditions get lost in translation
but I'm a refugee in my own country
where it's safe for some, but not for me.
I'm trying to blend in.
It's not possible to translate what I know into English.
I wasn't pulled, but was pushed.
No one asked me who I was.
I didn't grieve the loss of my hand-made home
but I left everything I knew.
I'm from behind the mountains I once loved.
Now I'm outside my country and
would like to go to Canada.
If you knock on my gate
at two in the morning, come in
to the crowded single room of poetry,
into this dining room, bedroom and kitchen,
everyone telling their story at the same time.

Places don't always travel with people
but the place that held my attention
for half my life still aggravates a flow
of associations. And when I write out
the points of entry into that discursive
instability, I remember those places as
the sites of danger. I think of the duplicity
of landscape images and text, those
photos of old men fishing, the paintings
and clever songs about place and
what is described in what follows—
the becoming, and then the disappearing,
the whirlpool in the center of the story of
the construction of locally produced landscape.
I put a river on a map. I can talk with conviction
about the Upper Nass. My home in Prince George
isn't large or secluded. I live among the poor.
In my early days on the Nass, I spent much
of my time looking for food until I escaped.

I'm a powerful, heavy-set man in my sixties.
I don't give orders. I used to drink myself stupid
and wander through the towns looking lost.
But at least I quit the timber trade when young.
I never lived in a boomtown but I know
the best wood goes to America and the worst
to the locals. The mills I saw bought wood
until there wasn't any more worth buying.
They like to buy logs from the flats by the rivers.
Companies narrate the places and histories.
There's never enough labour out there, so
they build a bunch of shacks and bring workers in.
After a while the mill closes down, the owners sell
the scraps, and some of the people stay. Most of
the men hunt and fish until there's nothing left,
and then they pack up and head to the city.

My territory belongs to the imagination.
New laws can't change it.
There's a bottleneck to the pipelines
in my roadless area.
The spruce and hemlock old growth stands
at the headwaters of the Nass
are as large as roaded West Virginia.
The vanishing frontier is a myth
you can read about in the founding texts
of the white man and pulp factories of the west.
Rayon's the product of American history.
Clear-cuts wipe out landscapes
before they become places
and the raw materials in the colonies
are turned into homogenized play lists
the moment the board feet are sold.

In the beginning was the noun, followed
by some numbers. Only viruses survive,
and beliefs are a kind of virus.
Beliefs, rumour, and copycat strategies
are perfect examples, but the idea
you won't have problems is a bad theory.
I was born here in the village
valences where empty forms
materialize. Turn here driver,
this is the pre-lingual place,
an old forest on an island
that isn't what it was.
Watch out for the corners.
My smaller language isn't spoken much
beyond my home.
Before roads, my language moved inland.
I didn't choose it. It chose me.
My nation gathers at the inlet
to mass and crowd beneath a tree,
to assemble into company.
But I'm not a prisoner of the poems of confinement.
Buildings on hills, as invisible as laws.
What does not change
is the archives, but the ears have walls.
It's control but they call it transparency
and the prison is open to the public.
The narrative goal being not closed circuit
confinement, but keeping danger out.

Poems flow toward consciousness.
A poem is an amplifier of information
that is not a continuous series of images
but a grainy wave
transmitted in packages of possibilities.
The implicate order of a poem
connects everything with everything.
Once two subversive poems have interacted
they can respond to each other's rhythms
thousands of years later.
This liminal signaling is faster than the speed of light.
Poems cause no conflict with reality.
The hiddeness of an unread poem
has to do with deeper reflections of reality.
Any individual element in a poem reflects
information on every other element in the poem.
Two waves in the same poem will interfere with each other
and create an audible pattern.
The laws of poetry are discontinuity and non-locality.
The layers of a poem go deeper and deeper
until the unknown.

I can't really say what I know
but I write provisional inferences
and, like others, perpetuate copies.
I don't know what's going on.
From simple beginnings, the poem
works in reverse through generations,
fibers meet just below the retina,
and perceptions shift. I don't care
about what's in the blind spot. At first
I saw animal faces in the trees, then
ambiguous figures moving off. That's
how it goes. Ordinarily, I'm not aware.
I don't know why we're alive.
There's always a rivalry wherever
I've gone, and the same old forces,
the same incompatible images involving
fears that can never be erased
suppress the imagination over time.
But I'm not locked on to metaphor
or what someone else says is the truth,
even though I'll remember the suffering
and fear and pain of poverty forever.

Listen, it's my two cents. If you don't like it,
keep the change, but if you're not willing
to risk everything and you're afraid
you will lose your social life and be assigned
a low language prestige like I was,
then write it off as a performance error.
I wanted to write in my own language.
Me, I'm like Honda. Pull hard, come easy,
like they say. I was born elsewhere
and I don't speak the official language.
English is the official language of the USA
but other languages are spoken where
I live. I live a low status on the shores
of a small island, an individual not in
the urban network, not in the same speech
community as the speakers of the urban
dialect. I don't speak their mother tongue
but one of the many languages of the Nass.
Hazelton is a case (see Loring and Lee) but
here, and in the UK and the USA, the choice
of a teaching model excludes the variety on
which they live. The English they teach is a
Foreign language. I'm not as careful as that.

I was sacrificed in politics on a sloping floor.
If I could close my eyes to the gap
between ourselves and livestock and
the billions of animals in factory farms
could stand their bloody ground;
and the bloodlines of the animals
who are not useful to men meant more
than mere lives that may be killed,
and if all life was evident—if the trade
in heads was no longer, if hooks
would straighten out and we would
not just protect and give prizes to
the safe, but make flourish poets of
resistance one again, then the power
to allow life would extend to all living
beings, but in the narrative, the means
are justified and called necessary suffering.
Everybody talks about stories
but nobody remembers them long.
I have a little black bag I wear on my back.
An outlaw, my story was killed
without sacrifice. More human than divine,
I am not a man and I live between the forest
and the city. I think the way animals think.

Sometimes it's hard to tell the difference
between a word and a decision.
Understandings accumulate.
There are bindings between words,
a kind of retrieval of memory traces.
First I saw distant lightning,
then heard what I thought was thunder,
then trees coming down, a chain reaction.
New meanings fold into the interchange.
Word or part word, poetry isn't always
an act of understanding. Consciousness
is an episodic series of moments but narrative isn't
necessarily consciousness. Fix saw, cut pole,
sometimes there's a darkness in the brain.
There's something beyond what can be grasped
even in poetry, beyond the list of words
that do not appear. Subjects discriminate,
and there's an infinite variety of forms
in the background feedback cycle of cues.

Hundreds of broken umbrellas lay around
and my ivy was foraging for light.
Meanings change and seeds land
where they can, but someone has
to feed the molds, to toss the slime
a few flakes of oats while the serious
vertebrates, who see nature as spectacle,
go on scheming in language. A biscuit
would be nice but I don't want one.
You get uneasy about taking tiny creatures
seriously when the conversation shifts,
but there's no clear border. Everything
transforms, but how? Hunger tightens
consciousness to the short form, ripples
criss-cross the slime's body, as if vegetables
are brains. Language has animal prejudices.
I like it here. I'm not trapped in old buildings.   †

---

†   Sponges are animals without a brain.
†   What follows from the disposition is
          intelligence doesn't need a brain.

Rocks sparkle and the well water rises
when the carriers awaken. That's when
the bonds are open and the lights begin
to sing, when they rise from the ground
like flames and are seen on ridges
and at sea. Movement leads to stress.
Full of flaws, forms are imperfect states
and deform when pushed against another.
It's never far from one side to the other.
Either the brittle bodies begin to move,
or the flow through the forms becomes
entangled, and locks and ends. When
existing knowledge becomes unstable
and currents that did not flow before
are flowing in the ground, when
the capillaries of porous bodies swell, and
the non-believers are somewhere in transition,
currents flow along the surface
and overwhelm the others that flow below.
One partner becomes reduced,
and the other is lost in information,
and someone asks a question about conversions
about how love spreads across the dirty surfaces.
Once we were non-conductors,
but now currents flow through the rock
and we are generated, arriving at the surface,
where impact occurs.

Choices have to be made but chances are
too good to miss. So often it's either too soon
or too late, but then there's a moment when
everything comes together, when sensations arrive
on top of each other, third party robbers sit in
on operations, and writers paper over the gaps,
fitting jumble into story. Most of the time,
most of us live in a twilight zone of inklings.
There's no way of knowing the time it takes
for messages to travel from the land to the brain.
There's a delay—it takes time for creatures to travel—
differences collapse and ideas circulate slowly.
Accidents change things. Cross-signal events
affect survival, and self-publishing changes
the feed. Memory, backdated illusions smeared out
in time, varies from person to person, the pixels
break down, and the motion gets jerky.

This is not my own, and my center is somewhere else.
Poetry is not a serious business, and not an idle pleasure.
If my life were free of demands, I might find no need
for poetry, but schools generate dissatisfactions:
The travellers for pleasure become the subject.
I'm interested in anything that moves away from place,
a change of location. The poems I look for are not
taken in by landscape and the make-believe, for
the real is too disgusting and meaning is
a limited place with hunts for persuasive events.
Place ends at the center of culture.
I don't look for meaning in the poems of others.
The awkward movement of an injured arm swaps place
for loose change. In fact, poetry is not enjoyable
but can regenerate hope from fatigue. It is legitimate
debauchery, an escape from boredom into forgetfulness.
This is why the poetry I make is full of immediate diversions
and is mostly meaningless. I can say this because I am
not institutionalized and have no center. Poetry is caused
by a push, not by the pull of place. I like to get away to
a reading, but I'm also a peasant, and peasants travel little.

I was too poor to want to go camping.
Meaning resists definition but land came to mean
repression and animal slaves, so I migrated from
the rural north to the urban south. Since then,
I don't go to, or through parks. It's not my territory.
There's too much potential for conflict in them
because the residents hold the place attachments
of imposing men. They build their houses on land
in the city, then they get land vehicles, and then
they return to the land of their birth, the land
of make-believe, the untroubled land of reason.
My land is unknown land, any ground, meadow
or woods. I won't be going back to the river
and I'm growing onward without it. I don't love
those places or groups seeking meaning from
the environment in places with the landscape
preference some call leisure differences. But
education is not the diviner of meaning. This
is about the variables of meaning, about writing
impressions on an affected landscape of place
attachments ripped from white-page phone books.
I wanted to live where there's no work on the land,
where the land had never been plowed.

The river where I lived was small enough
for wolves to wade the tailouts, but
I never thought of it as skinny water. In fact,
it wasn't much different from the Amazon.
Watersheds and definitions are similar,
and I did little with the land. There was
more timber and as many fish as one
could want. The work was exhausting
but I learned to make long distance trades
and create new understandings. We made
a camp on a low bluff where old growth
trees fell into the river and chunks of
the cutbank washed out to the coast.
It wasn't long before I learned glamour
is the gloss on capital. After fifteen years,
I borrowed some money to buy a motor
for a boat. I worked in the transnational
commodity circuits. Now I have nothing
to cut, nothing to grow. I don't need wood
any more. I climbed the tallest trees to
look around. There are no more next
rivers. Each representation is more remote
than the one before. I cut my own routes.
The old growth was my warehouse and
I knew where I wanted to go from the start.
Individuals travel with their stories, and
I had some luck, cut the trees, and carried
out the pieces for our home on my back.

I didn't get anything by money or birth
and I had no land, but wanted some, so
I put up a little house around the corner.
Later now, I think place is limited to
a representation of nature. In fact I'd say
it's the prison of the local. Places assume
the particular through a shrewd cutting,
the transnational movement of forests.
It's not just outsiders like me who dip
a basket in the river, imagining potential.
But local has no meaning when the timber
runs out. There's no mystery in a dry sink.
One hand washes the other. I traded shakes
for food with partners up and down the river,
and later, lived in the old growth culture
of the Nass, sometimes sleeping in the open.
But my past is shared, and a story exists
to be told, and told again. I write
in a masculine idiom with regional roots,
but for thirty years I worked without the flavour
of sentiment, writing in invisible ink, living
on an invisible river. I've not heard of anyone
who rose above class without compromise.
Isn't it sad how the hick is always awkward
in the narrative of eviction? Shame is the shit
on the blanket of the local, but I remember
the moment I caught the bus out of town while
the locals stood in line and tried to fix the moment.

Even machines suffer from the hands of users.
They get run in the non-stop mode
until something breaks.
Meaning isn't reliable either.
It breaks down often and
failure rates increase with time.
Storms reduce the up-time,
mean time is downtime.
When external disturbances
like accidents are dominant,
no good predictions can be achieved.
Failures oscillate around words.
Excluded for most of my life,
I lost out for different reasons
but generally it's called the income gap.
This failure law describes distribution—
I travel less far and less often
but I also recover more quickly.

The same ideas seem more likely now
as we move toward completion at the end
of our cycle, when time speeds up and
boundaries dissolve. An occluded line
grazer, an all-at-once animal beyond
syntax in the liminal slime, I'm drawn
toward you through time, to all the last things,
and all the lost things. Why all this talk?
The phone rings in the middle of the night
but I don't answer. No one's ever there.
An updated node and ball too small to see,
when I rearrange my room, interference
patterns and three dimensional images
reflect living forms. Telephone used to
be a noun made by combining forms
but it's a verb now. You are not here,
and you are nowhere, and I wonder
if that coherent beam outside my door
is you, casting your shadow in.

The size of everything is increasing,
including rulers. It's called inflation
but it's like driftwood on the tide.
The twist of the story is, I make my own
measurements. When you became
the constant in my life, the world I knew
changed. I think I had fallen toward
the middle, that I had forgotten
about the strength of interactions.
If you want to know what really happened,
I was writing a code of narrow, black lines.
Now I know there are emission and
absorption lines, many possible worlds,
many random uncertainties.
Now I know there's an abundance
of answers, an archive of questions,
an infinite ladder of turbulent transitions.

Three. A door opens, causing mischief,
but it's not as bad as it looked at first.
The logical hierarchy doesn't make sense
by itself and I'll bet if we just stopped
for a minute, we could find a better idea
as soon as tomorrow morning, but
the recessive properties of the need
for believing whatever we like or buy
is a coding of sequences, and it's enough
to keep us busy until then. It's why
theories and syntax can't be trusted, why
we make the same mistakes over and over.
This is a brutal version of democracy
and it doesn't work. Remove a symbol,
remove a product, the greatest want is rigour.
Stealing words from the waste basket, I'm
the remainder of a division and I live among
decaying ideas, but I don't believe in Abalonia.

Faults can occur anywhere.
Things get out of step.
Promiscuous forms cycle upward
when something isn't right.
Blackouts cascade, texts slide
under other texts, and always,
master narrative railroad fictions
grind along the North American fault line.
Faults break up lines.
There's pressure along the edges,
corruption between the lines.
Animals start my thoughts
and I think of the plot against them.
Competition is a blood noun, syntax
a breadcrumb trail. Camp
was a cleared space
concentrated around the corner.
If grouse wandered into camp,
they were killed. They were trusting and
indifferent to experience.
The bigger the balls, the smaller the brain.
No one talks about the blind spot.
Animals matter but men remain silent
and use every trick in the book
to destroy the living and
keep animals on their plates.

They put me to work on shore, grabbing and landing the hens.
I brought fish to my lure but had no hook. It is easy to imagine
the steelhead among the boulders. I charmed them but
did not deceive them. I awakened their curiosity but I did
not chase them. I drew them from their hiding places
and soothed them. I brought them close so I could see them,
but I would not provoke the hen so I could hook the buck.
I would not need the techne reel and carried no gadgets.
In high water I saw them in the bush. They were love-sick
so I didn't tease them or rip their lips. Fishermen brag
about their hot hens. And they brag about their technology.
The photos degrade the fish, especially the hero shot.
Steelhead are the most vulnerable to men.
Mimicry, language and gadgets are their tools of the slaughter.
The focus is mostly on the men and their desire
and little is on the fish. The fish is just a thing but
at the same time the men seek to experience the life
of the fish. The fish experiences the hard hand of the fisher, and
just as in hate and sex crimes, apathy and empathy are there.

It is medicinal to see a wild steelhead,
although you should not drink their water.
I lived beside a river in a place that was an object
where the subject had too much to do.
Fishing is about travel and consumption of the excessive.
It is an unnecessary pleasure
reinforced by writers who read water.
The best rivers are authorized by enforcement.
There is no universal stare that is true for all anglers.
There are those who can, and those who cannot,
but the professional classes began to believe
standing in the rivers was to do one good.
Place is where one works, but when I go away
I anticipate I will see a river from a road.
For sure to take the waters is to take the cure
because a river is a place of medicine more than pleasure.
To have been on the Damdochax for a week
is better than an eternity on the Nechako.
It is good to wade wild waters and even the Sustut will do.
Swimming in the river does one good.
During September there is an increase in river swimming
although really it is more immersion than swimming.
Springs on the beach are best left for sockeye.

Travel books destroy rivers.
Undamaged steelhead are a snob good
not unlike a good book.
One is good and two is better.
This is about the overcrowded view of water.
All it takes is a split second.
Steelhead are never numerous
and so are caught again and again.
In fishing, as one consumes more, another consumes less.
Wild steelhead in wild places are scarce
and the guides are the old masters.
Rivers are places of wonder, visited places
having to do with relational consumption.
Cheap travel means no more undisturbed places
so I left it for the travellers.
I imagine the end of supply.
I didn't make a good guide
because I didn't fit the purpose
and smashed my good future.
Fly fishing is an affordable pleasure
and I had no good explanation at night
for the mess we made each day,
but the romantic gaze is persuasive
and men are suckered in by fantasies.
My guests came from good families and I did not.
The catch is expensive and the release in good taste.
The Blackwater is good to look at
and has been a good investment for my daughter.

I see good in what she is doing.
She has made good on her promise and pays the money on time.
The Blackwater is worth having.
My ex is well behaved and obedient on the river and I was not.
Back then I took the good with the bad.
Some of the assholes were always good for a laugh.
I wasn't very good at casting but the river was good to me.
In the winter months I helped the bourgeois
organize their thoughts and make decisions.
On the river I gave good advice.
Now I get up when I'm good and ready and not before.
I'm better off now. The fact is, I never had it so good.

I trust, not in men or their systems,
but in women, and I don't care about
saving time, or covering more space.
Writing of cities is about power
and class, and poems about place
are towns that look alike. The only
thing that differentiate them is
the memories in the buildings of authority,
where memory is manufactured,
and time is not money, but space.
When we remember together, other
memories are silenced and called heritage
in the space of a few hours, broadcast
into every room until the storage capacity
is full. Clock time is something signaling
the total, but the way I remember, what
I heard was about the succession
of forms and temporal complexity.
Anyway, I was distracted and inattentive,
and looking for some breathing space,
an opening or break, something I could
say in the company of strangers.

For thirty summers in a row I flew north
to the Damdochax where the weather
warms to mild and the sand is dirty.
It doesn't matter where it is,
in Gitxsan it's called paradise.
Place means something to Wii Minosik,
but it doesn't to the drifters.
It doesn't matter where they go.
The beach is not a place and
they'd sooner travel to another
state of mind than a different spot.
But then, their ritual subjects
were diversions I did not stop for.
Going to the same spot the next day,
going to a different spot, the next day,
the same. The next wave, so many
living things in the transition. The
more shared, the fewer convergences.
Through small departures, the force
of simplification wears all that is made
into a simpler form. Body waves and
time scales happen to matter.
I grew up in an atmosphere that was
connected to the past. Water is a
true transient and my annual spring flight
north was a flow pathway in a field
setting somehow like ground truthing.

The home of verifiable intelligence
is south of the border
but the water issues here,
where the coordinates are zero.
Oh indicative, evocative clever dream,
there's no virtue in your sentiment.
Tomorrow is before the end of time
so in the present, give the world to come
the sympathy of provenance and affinity
and after the wind has died away,
be in the give, for natural is not inborn
and not within reason, but a lyric
of distribution and supply
in which the common harmony
is contained within the present.

Landscape is about something
but it is not of something I know.
The quiet and peaceful views
in poems made of everyday objects
are a background for something
else, narratives or evocative stories
suitable for replay, and they are about
the ideal game and the never-ending
story. It's the reason some games
are played and some are not.
The narrative is about conspiracies,
cover-ups, land disputes and violence.
Landscape isn't nature and
landscape art is what farmers see.
That something should be done
about a landscape that is separated
by fences is one of the reasons
for this. When nature is the image
and the object is the landscape,
everything resembles everything
else. It is often the view through
a window. Realistic landscape is
an escape that happens when
country becomes leisure landscape.

Things come and go. Logs go out and cows go in.
Cheap meat's in the cards on the roads of colonization.
Eventually the north will be a tribal area the size of London
because cattle come and lumber goes.
Chicago fought the wilderness and lost,
now the forest's dying on its own.
And the trade winds are weakening, a fact
to do with pig iron, sugar cane and charcoal.
I wish I had a ticket that would get me out
of the agro-industrial western front.
If I was released into the wild, I'd go
to a place without bushmeat and primate pets.
The order of things isn't like walking into a hotel room
and change through politics is an illusion.
I'm a landless leftover and I'm back from the dead
but this time when I'm gone, I'm gone for good.

Everything about place is depleted over time.
It's too late to go to the US, but the up and
down mixing of the tedious subject of place
perpetuates the storybook flow of segregation
and indifference. For many years I have
been fascinated by revised editions, how
writing anything about exotic destinations
consumes old places. It's why I'm not mobile.
There's nothing to look at here, not much reason
for visitors to come. It hasn't always been so,
but now when the reader is a visitor and
the poet is the local, the massive flow
of images transforms to (1) cheap goods
driving prices down, (2) cross-border
takeovers. It's too bad, but there are
no entry restrictions on the rural idyll.

Up is north and now that I'm older
and more complex, more close
to the rising and the setting—
there are two countries, one
at the top edge of the map,
the other at the bottom.
When the current increases,
so does the field, and the spin
of bodies and waves in the night sky
are landmarks used for direction.
If you go up the river
until you come to the end of it,
then go down the valley where
the water flows the other way
for a long time, you will see
what I mean. I was repelled
by other things and you, a primary
direction in the form of a turning
point, were an outside influence
that flipped my poles.

A line is a time arrow—the line returns
when a vase falls and breaks. The shorter the line,
the more precise the location, but the greater
the distribution. The longer the line, the longer the waves,
and the more the vase energy is evenly distributed.
The past loves misery. Many misunderstandings
make up the past. Love is many noded and
all the lines that pierce it are experiments
of one kind or another. The length of love is related
to the strength of the bounce. Everything is
made of pieces and I am like a piece of cloth
woven out of threads. The lines join the nodes
and the faces join together and we share a common
face. There is no water between the molecules
of water, no time between the ticks of time.
Nowhere is the same as it was a hundred years ago
but I still move around and light moves through.

Embryo's are the raw material.
Ransom assembled the first lines
and changed the way things were made—
the interchangeable parts
and continuous flow
of the first moving line
in a meat packing house
inspired mass production.
It's called curricula now
but grain rolled off the belt back then.
One job ends and another begins.
Now they call invisible work, natural work
because it makes sense
but it isn't worth anything.
Today's plant workers
don't plant crops or cook
and only the hardest workers remember
what was drilled into them
on the assembly line
before the work began to move
and the titles went out of print.

But I was thinking of what is
so quickly forgotten, how time and again
few speak of this preoccupation
with genre decorum, how
there's no meaning, but in things.
And I was thinking of the pictures we point to
and the fugitive activity of mind,
of the patronage of the public
I ought to be abandoning, that
I should break away from
because landscape changes
and imaginative writing wears thin.
In the end I would like to thank the Stanley foundation
and Wii Minosik and Niist for their permission
while I was working out my debts,
on my way from chaos, to unity, to the plural,
working out of my displaced aspirations,
my enquiry into the origins of the idea of the beautiful,
by no means an account of European settlements.

The land lies open—shallow water sites occur
where the land lies low. Much of the eroded land
lies on the southern slope where it is warmer
and drier. The value of this now vacant land
lies in development potential. It is sown for
one or two years, and then the land lies fallow
until it is overgrown with wild grasses.
Natural land lies beyond the fringe, the forest
land lies in the middle part of the slope,
common land lies north of the city's roads,
and my land lies along the river. Almost all
land lies. The future of the land, and
the ultimate responsibility for restoring the
disturbed land lies with companies from
the south who have been peering between
the peaks to look at how the land lies. There
are at least 50 land lies. The flat land lies.
Most of the abandoned farm land lies in the
hills, but only 16 percent of all inhabited land
lies below 100 meters. All the agricultural
land lies. The price of land lies around 8.7.
My dead reckoning is usually good enough
to tell me in which direction the land lies.
Much of the remaining land lies in marginal
areas or in the abundantly forested regions.
Near vast bodies of water, land lies parched.
There are stands of old-growth trees
within the clear-cut swathe, and the disputed

land lies across the settled side. The thrust
of neo-classical conception of urban land
lies in treating it as a commodity which
is governed by microeconomic laws. But,
in effect, behind the redistribution of
land lies, is the redistribution of income, the
redistribution of opportunity, and the denial
of dispossession from the land lies before
Israel. Not enough land lies idle, and there's
too much information about the direction
in which cultivable and company land lies.

In my early years I kept animal skins,
and when we cleared a garden,
the reading of unoccupied land
came into being through praxis and was called place.
The power of the river attracted my curiosity
so we fished, picked berries and cut timber,
leaving landmarks that fell into the river
of the Lissims Arcadia, where I still have access,
but no longer have the land.
I am the dead husband,
but this is no way to think about my husband
and what he made in the Nass.
This is not another account of land violence.
This was once open water,
but now grizzlies shuffle in the swales.
I handed over my ties to the modern world
when I first went to the Damdochax.
There wasn't enough flat ground
to find a place to sleep.
It's not another story of betrayal
about the transformation of nature.
People locate themselves in their stories of place.
I lived at a place that fell out of the local.
Even now, ten years after I sold it, I still have it.

Colonies swarm, fish school, patterns
of motion appear out of nowhere.
Humans need language to organize
but most align with ignorance.
In the mind of the swarm, behaviour
changes from chaos to order and
we move along the migration routes
with the direction of local rules,
a driver's manual and desire.
The larger the group, the fewer the
leaders needed. Everyone disagrees
on who the experts are
but it's too late to control us
once we start marching.

America is inadequate and stumbles in
and stumbles out of repetitive errors
called wars. And America is physically
unready, but like they say, whatever
is, will be more there, and so it is it will
not die until wars end. But the fibers
that carry signals carry a hint of what
lies ahead, like faces in the clouds, and
when events correspond, and swindlers
fill in the blanks, most won't know if
America went business class or tourist.
Chance works, but when history repeats
itself, the US won't see the world that way,
and won't correspond to anything, going back
for more contraptions and speed, remembering
the beautiful idea, which appeared early.

We don't know enough
about side effects
but housing and care
and the demand for new drugs
are convergents, like asthma
and guinea pigs.
Anything goes when
the animals don't behave.
Science works within the law
but that doesn't mean it's right.
Bypass dead ends and help
rescue the sick from hospitals.
Animals are poor models and
the numbers are thrown away.
Even if the cages are clean
and there's enough water,
eventually it's time
for research.

Last year's bridge beams
slow this year's water
in the tangled roots
of the toppled trees.
Each flood they skid
a riffle downstream.
The habitats are complex and wild
and bridge beams make more fish.
Some live in the root balls,
some in the leaves,
some among the branches,
some in hollow trees.

Some say animals live at the bottom. They say
inequality is necessary, and resist interest
in the question about having to start over,
but animals are not tools, not to be used.
Numbers dwindle as one gets further away
from averages, and the reality is,
long poems do not signify more poetry.
Nothing I know of is ever a perfect curve.
There's always an interview before the cut.
Experience is content and content's the difference.
The distribution of poetry across the land
has consequences. Some poems make decisions,
some don't. Sometimes foods are too hard
to open and suggestions are repressed.
Animals think thoughts without words, and
when an animal feels afraid, and they know
what they like and what they dislike,
I hear your footsteps coming to my door
and I know you have found your way.

Animals fit but humans are the animal that doesn't fit.
Animals get along without us. Humans are only one
of many animals that ignore words, although some of us
put off completing sentences for as long as we can.
All animals hope for good news. Sooner or later
everyone surprises everyone. Animals use sticks.
Every human has been humiliated by an animal.
All animals have animal minds. Animals know
the difference between important and urgent.
Only humans punish themselves. All animals
rub their skins against each other. It's OK
for a while and then it's too much. Animals hear
the screams in Prince George. Humans shave
the hair in their ears. Animals make guesses
that are accurate. Human correspondence is never
exact, and the distance between the ears has
nothing to do with it. Animals know when
they have a problem. Only humans check
for mail twice in a row. Language dogs know
the longer the delay, the more the mail.
Humans who check all the time get nothing.

Stepping out on mounds and
over the pits is
life in the trees,
in the layers of the Nass.
There are no stone walls or wire
choking elders
in the understory where
faces begin, the familiar
faces in the forest—
in the lichens and
moss, on the fallen
logs and snags, growing on
the limbs and rocks
in the bogs and marl and
salt, in the cord grass and chicken claws
of this ragged canopy.

In the understory, loosening the Minnesota forest floor,
the European earthworm hitches a ride north
in bait boxes. In the subplot radius,
random lines indicate positions
in the form of visible leading edges.
Plots are vacant circles made of men
or mean errors known as empty squares.
Able to control the composition of communities,
invaders represent a shift in synthesis.
They are everything that can be fitted
into a parenthesis, measured relationships
at opposite ends but an exclosure is everything else
so don't dump your bait on shore.

The extra dimensions come as a surprise
the instant the reader gets pulled in—
the spiral reaches all the way
in the actual moment they're read.
Strands of stars and swaths of dust!
It's a three braner but
the flavour structure is anyone's guess.
It all began in a bar called the milky way.
The form of a poem changes over time.
Poems can be cannibalistic and merge
with their neighbours. The city limits
are over the horizon. I make the trip,
but I'm tired when I get there.

I am not my body. I got it from the animals.
I'm animal headed, not all that special,
a caribou on a stick. When animals unite
for play, D is for the door they close
when they post sentries for the night
while ganglions on Nikes cycle by,
sequences with bacteria. Fishing is interference
and I would look without interfering
because I know we can turn into one another—
a bear is a marmot is a fisher is a wren.
Desire is the filling of nouns and civilization is
the merchandise of the fake. Nothing is fixed,
nothing's according to instructions. I call it
Brian's razor, but other explanations exist.
I'm against Brian's razor.
Simple poems or lines are not more likely to be true
than complex. Then parsimony became known as
another Canon, and the cries of animals
were denied. Professions fill the meaning gap.
They keep the dissatisfaction going
and stay with the hurt. Knowledge grows awkwardly,
then when you die, you lose everything.

Cultures are infectious—talking or sneezing,
the same common paths of thought.
Sea lice going back and forth between
wild and hatchery fish. But now,
the thoughts you got from others
don't have me anymore. I got the idea
I could go to work for myself from another
and I'm glad I quit before my mind was eaten up
by social contact while I slept.
Now I'm no longer buried alive in local history
between those old time groupings.
It's called live and learn and I'm lucky.
I'm not making it up
but I get my information for free.
New forms are created deep down in time
when all the cages are released
and we're at the time of a shift.
My refrigerator magnets drop off
and deer come down from the mountain.
Next time I go back to watch the creep
I'm going to clean my house
and open the window a day early.

And I seemed not of them
or yourself with the rain,
not of the storm,
not of the calm,
but the boatman's chant
when the end is near
and no more will be known.
Persist then, when nothing can,
when the living condition
running through the story
shifts between
the hopefulness of rhythmic motion
and the growth of matter
stirred up into storms.

There are weak forces and strong forces
and there will be an end to our lives—
done video, done audio, done by done.
Make sure the roads can handle the load
for the body is the force carrier
and all the relinquished reminders of the body,
and the very people will be done;
but when's not a question to be asked of trees.
When shop for its all about is done,
and the attempts at unification of the body are done,
when the intentions expire, I won't be like me.

Ever since avatars became dominant at the turn
of the century I like to wander around in the stores
to look at things that might still be there.
No archivist, I write in interpreted language,
which can mean making a new environment
for an existing game. I'm a soy boy scattering
unknown titles and the game line gives me
the rights of distribution. When I'm out
wandering with the brutality of chance,
cheap access isn't possible. Rhetoric reverses
when the sites are going down and
everything gets trickier than you think.
The content side might not cut it.
The more you lose, the harder the game gets.
I play free games. Coincidence provides
in my play brain and I like taking it
into my own hands. Sometimes I behave
as one, and sometimes the other.

You never know what you're going
to face. Last night the crowd
was unforgiving. I don't know
how to serve in that feeling
but tonight the waiting dance clicks.
Monday I knew the agony of serving
the so-called smart people. Tuesday
I spat in your coffee because
you deserved it. Wednesday
you asked for a refill. Last night
was the night of a hundred tables
but tonight it's slow and the hours
are flexible. Last night I wanted to sit in
but there were no available seats.
Tonight the tables have turned.
Last night I survived food, tonight
I dish it out and fetch the extra
dressing. Last night I lost forks
when you came in, tonight
you leave my table smiling.

I camped on the beach of the river. B is for
bank where the land sloped to the water
where I watched slime cross the stream
on a cottonwood log-near the bearing tree
at the headwaters of the Slamgeesh.
But everything has intentions and I was
reminded of a dream—even though at
any moment an answer can come, it will
probably remain a secret. You should not
know everything. Who knows what
the Jays have in mind? I stood still
in the river for years. At every bend
I walked across, stepping on every rock,
and yet the fish went to unknown places.
Cotton grass grew in the glade.
Jays listen to adults and practice on
their own, remembering their mothers
in the vegetal tapestry. Everything abstracts.

This is the story that ends with
an o, the one where I cut myself
free with a chainsaw, a sequel
of blood for the subject's sake,
starting out when I'm on my way
back to the beginning, a splatter
poem where the subject survives
and everyone knows it's you.
The blood of the narrative flows
over the text, and writers string
special effects together and call it
plot, a fragmented representation
about the horror of our lives,
everyone picking over the bones,
neighbours scared after the story,
living with the fear of shapes
shifting, the unnamable thing.

I would like to thank the BC Arts Council for a writing grant, allowing me the time to assemble much of this book.

Older versions of some of the sequences herein were previously published in *West Coast Line*, the chap book *when snakes awaken* (Nomados Literary Publishers), *Event Magazine*, the Fort St John Poetics Research Group web journal *Treeline*, *George Street Letters* and Louis Cabri's *The Transparency Machine*. Some were also read on CBC Radio.

This book was set with Kennerley Old Style from P22 Font Foundry. Kennerley was originally designed by Goudy for publisher Mitchell Kennerley in 1911. Goudy described it as a "book letter with strong serifs, firm hairlines, and makes a solid, compact page." Recognized as one of Goudy's best text faces, Kennerley is considered an original American classic as it is not based on historical type designs.